READ
ME
POETRY

I'll Tell You A Story
And Other Story Poems

Acknowledgements

Every effort has been made to obtain permission to reproduce copyright material but there may be cases where we have been unable to trace a copyright holder. The publisher apologizes for any such error and will be happy to correct any omission in future printings.

"The Sound Collector" by Roger McGough. © 1990 Roger McGough. Reprinted by permission of PFD on behalf of Roger McGough

"One Dark Night" by Richard Edwards from TEACHING THE PARROT. Reprinted by permission of the publisher, Faber & Faber Ltd

"A Pig Tale" from COMPLETE POEMS FOR CHILDREN. © James Reeves. Reprinted by permission of the James Reeves Estate

"Fairy Story" by Stevie Smith. Reprinted by permission of the Executors of James MacGibbon

"Three Birds Flying" by Eve Merriam from OUT LOUD by Eve Merriam. © 1973 Eve Merriam, © renewed 2001 Dee Michel and Guy Michel. Used by permission of Marian Reiner

"Nicholas Naylor" by Charles Causley from COLLECTED POEMS FOR CHILDREN published by Macmillan. Reprinted by permission of David Higham Associates

"A Good View of the Sea" by Geoffrey Summerfield. © The Estate of Geoffrey Summerfield

"The Silver Penny" by Walter de la Mare. © Walter de la Mare. Reprinted by permission of the Literary Trustees of Walter de la Mare, and the Society of Authors as their Representative

"The Black Pebble" from COMPLETE POEMS FOR CHILDREN. © James Reeves. Reprinted by permission of the James Reeves Estate

"Night Flight" by Shirley Hughes from RHYMES FOR ANNIE ROSE published by Bodley Head. Reprinted by permission of Random House, UK

"Poem" from COLLECTED POEMS by Langston Hughes published by Vintage. Reprinted by permission of David Higham Associates

First published 2001 by Walker Books Ltd
87 Vauxhall Walk, London SE11 5HJ

This edition published 2007 for Index Books Ltd

4 6 8 10 9 7 5 3

This book has been typeset in Adobe Caslon

Printed in China

British Library Cataloguing in Publication Data:
a catalogue record for this book is
available from the British Library.

ISBN 978-0-7445-6884-4

www.walkerbooks.co.uk

I'll Tell You A Story
And Other Story Poems

Selected by Myra Barrs and Sue Ellis

Illustrated by Sue Heap

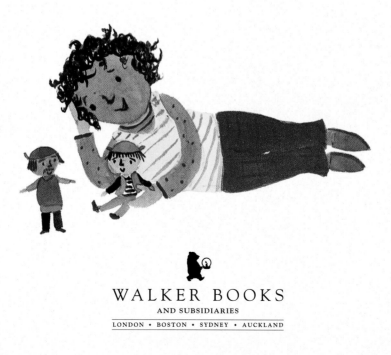

WALKER BOOKS
AND SUBSIDIARIES
LONDON · BOSTON · SYDNEY · AUCKLAND

I'll Tell You a Story

I'll tell you a story
About Jack a Nory,
And now my story's begun;
I'll tell you another
About Jack and his brother,
And now my story's done.

Traditional

WINDY NIGHTS

Whenever the moon and stars are set,
    Whenever the wind is high,
All night long in the dark and wet,
    A man goes riding by.
Late in the night when the fires are out,
Why does he gallop and gallop about?

Whenever the trees are crying aloud,
    And ships are tossed at sea,
By, on the highway, low and loud,
    By at the gallop goes he.
By at the gallop he goes, and then
By he comes back at the gallop again.

Robert Louis Stevenson

THE SOUND COLLECTOR

A stranger called this morning
Dressed all in black and grey
Put every sound into a bag
And carried them away

The whistling of the kettle
The turning of the lock
The purring of the kitten
The ticking of the clock

The popping of the toaster
The crunching of the flakes
When you spread the marmalade
The scraping noise it makes

The hissing of the frying-pan
The ticking of the grill
The bubbling of the bathtub
As it starts to fill

The drumming of the raindrops
On the window-pane
When you do the washing-up
The gurgle of the drain

The crying of the baby
The squeaking of the chair
The swishing of the curtain
The creaking of the stair

A stranger called this morning
He didn't leave his name
Left us only silence
Life will never be the same.

Roger McGough

Wah, wah!

Crunch!
Tick, tock!

Pop!
Squeak!

Swish!
Creak!

ONE DARK NIGHT

Little Granny Witherspoon
    was sitting, knitting, rocking,
When steps crunched on the path outside
    and someone started knocking,
"Now who on earth can that be
    on a night so wild and raw?"
Said Granny, shuffling down the hall
    towards her cottage door.

The stranger in the front porch grinned,
    "I wonder if I might
Just step inside to warm myself.
    It's bitter out tonight."
"Of course," said Granny. "Please, come in
    and shelter from the rain.
There, sit close to the fire, my dear.
    What was your name again?"

"My name? Er ... Wolf," the stranger answered,
    moving to a chair,
His jaw was long, he had a hungry look
    and thick grey hair.
"You'll have some tea," said Granny kindly.
    "Take this last cup, do,
While I pop to the kitchen
    and put on another brew."

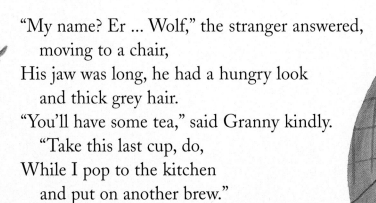

She left. The stranger licked his lips
   and raised the dainty cup,
He'd have his tea and then, perhaps,
   a snack to fill him up.
He sighed contentedly and sipped.
   He glanced around the room,
Then sat bolt upright ... thirteen wolf heads
   glared down from the gloom!

Yes, thirteen wolf heads, glass-eyed, varnished,
   stuffed and mounted, dead.
He sprang up from his chair to leave.
   "Don't go, dear," Granny said.
She looked so sweet in fluffy slippers,
   hair in a neat grey bun,
And holding – not a tray of tea and biscuits –
   but a gun...

The storm howls round the cottage walls,
   the wild winds sweep and moan,
But Granny in her tiny cottage
   never feels alone,
She turns the lights down, rakes the coals,
   whispers a quiet "Night night",
And fourteen wolf heads grin back
   in the embers' dying light.

Richard Edwards

A FARMER WENT TROTTING

A farmer went trotting upon his grey mare,
   Bumpety, bumpety, bump!
With his daughter behind him so rosy and fair,
   Lumpety, lumpety, lump!

   A raven cried, Croak! and they all tumbled down,
      Bumpety, bumpety, bump!
   The mare broke her knees and the farmer his crown,
      Lumpety, lumpety, lump!

The mischievous raven flew laughing away,
   Bumpety, bumpety, bump!
And vowed he would serve them the same the next day,
   Lumpety, lumpety, lump!

Traditional

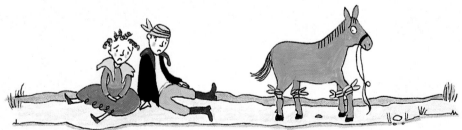

A Pig Tale

Poor Jane Higgins,
She had five piggins,
And one got drowned in the Irish Sea.

Poor Jane Higgins,
She had four piggins,
And one flew over a sycamore tree.

Poor Jane Higgins,
She had three piggins,
And one was taken away for pork.

Poor Jane Higgins,
She had two piggins,
And one was sent to the Bishop of Cork.

Poor Jane Higgins,
She had one piggin,
And that was struck by a shower of hail,

So poor Jane Higgins,
She had no piggins,
And that's the end of my little pig tale.

James Reeves

Mr East gave a feast;

Mr North laid the cloth;

Mr West did his best;

Mr South burnt his mouth

With eating a cold potato.

Traditional

THREE WISE MEN OF GOTHAM

Three wise men of Gotham

Went to sea in a bowl:

And if the bowl had been stronger,

My song would have been longer.

Traditional

OLD MOTHER HUBBARD

Old Mother Hubbard
Went to the cupboard,
To fetch her poor dog a bone;
But when she got there
The cupboard was bare
And so the poor dog had none.

She went to the baker's
To buy him some bread;
But when she came back
The poor dog was dead.

She went to the undertaker's
To buy him a coffin;
But when she came back
The poor dog was laughing.

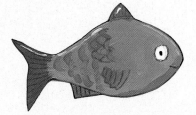

She went to the fishmonger's
To buy him some fish;
But when she came back
He was licking the dish.

She went to the fruiterer's
   To buy him some fruit;
But when she came back
   He was playing the flute.

She went to the tailor's
   To buy him a coat;
But when she came back
   He was riding a goat.

She went to the hatter's
   To buy him a hat;
But when she came back
   He was feeding the cat.

The dame made a curtsey,
   The dog made a bow;
The dame said, Your servant,
   The dog said, Bow-wow.

Traditional

ONE MISTY, MOISTY MORNING

One misty, moisty morning
When cloudy was the weather,
There I met an old man
Clothed all in leather;
Clothed all in leather,
With cap under his chin.
How do you do, and how do you do,
And how do you do again?

Traditional

THREE GHOSTESSES

Three little ghostesses,
Sitting on postesses,
Eating buttered toastesses,
Greasing their fistesses,
Up to their wristesses.
Oh, what beastesses
To make such feastesses!

Traditional

FAIRY STORY

I went into the wood one day
And there I walked and lost my way

When it was so dark I could not see
A little creature came to me

He said if I would sing a song
The time would not be very long

But first I must let him hold my hand tight
Or else the wood would give me a fright

I sang a song, he let me go
But now I am home again there is nobody I know.

Stevie Smith

THREE BIRDS FLYING

Once in a dream
there came to me
three birds flying
one, two, three.

The first was dark as water on a stone,

the second shone bright as sunlight on a stone,

and the third was grey as a stone, as a stone.

I rode with them
as they flew on,
but when I woke
the dream was gone.

I set it down on paper
and the words are there;
and every time I read it,
the birds are there.

Eve Merriam

NICHOLAS NAYLOR

Nicholas Naylor
The deep-blue sailor
Sailed the sea
As a master-tailor.

He scwcd for the Captain,
He sewed for the crew,
He sewed up the kit-bags
And hammocks too.

He sewed up a serpent,
He sewed up a shark,
He sewed up a sailor
In a bag of dark.

How do you like
Your work, master-tailor?
"So, so, so,"
Said Nicholas Naylor.

Charles Causley

THE SILVER PENNY

"Sailorman, I'll give to you
　　My bright silver penny,
If out to sea you'll sail me
　　And my dear sister Jenny."

"Get in, young sir, I'll sail ye
　　And your dear sister Jenny,
But pay she shall her golden locks
　　Instead of your penny."

They sail away, they sail away,
　　O fierce the winds blew!
The foam flew in clouds
　　And dark the night grew!

And all the green sea-water
　　Climbed steep into the boat;
Back to the shore again
　　Sail they will not.

Drowned is the sailorman,
　　Drowned is sweet Jenny,
And drowned in the deep sea
　　A bright silver penny.

Walter de la Mare

THE BLACK PEBBLE

There went three children down to the shore,
  Down to the shore and back;
There was skipping Susan and bright-eyed Sam
  And little scowling Jack.

Susan found a white cockle-shell,
  The prettiest ever seen,
And Sam picked up a piece of glass
  Rounded and smooth and green.

But Jack found only a plain black pebble
  That lay by the rolling sea,
And that was all that ever he found;
  So back they went all three.

The cockle-shell they put on the table,
  The green glass on the shelf,
But the little black pebble that Jack had found,
  He kept it for himself.

James Reeves

A GOOD VIEW OF THE SEA

There was an old man who climbed up a tree
Because he wanted to see the sea.

"Before I die, I want to see
The tumbling rumbling sea, you see."

So he climbed all day up the tallest tree,
And he stubbed a toe and he scrazed a knee.

The people said, "He'll run out of breath!"
"He'll tumble down!" "He'll catch his death!"

But when he reached the very top,
He said, "There's no more tree. I'll have to stop."

So he lodged himself on a wobbly branch,
Took out his bag, and ate his lunch.

Then he sat for an hour and looked for the sea
But the tide was out and all he could see

Was miles and miles of pebbles and sand:
Not a drop of sea at the edge of the land!

But he said, "No sweat! I'm in no hurry."
And soon the sea rushed back with a flurry.

And the waves came crashing on cliffs and in caves,
And sunlight shimmered on a million waves.

And he said as he sat in the top of the tree
"This tree is a wonderful place to be.

"I'll never go down. I'll join the birds.
It's so good up here, I'm lost for words."

Soon, people came from far and wide
To see him perch on the tree's topside.

They heard him twitter, they heard him coo,
And they threw him food, like at the zoo.

For the rest of his life, he stared at the sea
From the top of the tree, where he wanted to be.

And for the rest of his life he said not a word,
But cooed and twittered and sang like a bird!

Geoffrey Summerfield

NIGHT FLIGHT

Annie flew out of the window,
Bedclothes and cot and all,
And floated around above the ground,
And over the garden wall.

And her shadow skimmed over the gardens
And followed her all the way,
As she looked down on the roofs of the town
And the moon shone as bright as day.

Shirley Hughes